People of the Bible

The Bible through stories and pictures

King David

Copyright © in this format Belitha Press Ltd., 1986

Text copyright © Catherine Storr 1986

Illustrations copyright © Paul Crompton 1986

Art Director: Treld Bicknell

First published in the United States of America 1986
by Raintree Publishers Inc.
310 West Wisconsin Avenue, Milwaukee, Wisconsin 53203
in association with Belitha Press Ltd., London.

Conceived, designed and produced by Belitha Press Ltd.,
2 Beresford Terrace, London N5 2DH

ISBN 0-8172-2042-9 (U.S.A.)

Library of Congress Cataloging in Publication Data

Storr, Catherine.
    King David.

    (People of the Bible)
    Summary: David serves as a brave warrior in Saul's
armies against the Philistines, and after Saul's death
becomes King of Israel.
        1. David, King of Israel—Juvenile literature.
2. Bible. O.T.—Biography—Juvenile literature.
3. Israel—Kings and rulers—Biography—Juvenile
literature. [1. David, King of Israel. 2. Bible
stories—O.T.] I. Title. II. Series.
BS580.D3S693   1985   222′.409505   85-12284

ISBN 0-8172-2042-9

First published in Great Britain in paperback 1986
by Methuen Children's Books Ltd
11 New Fetter Lane, London EC4P 4EE

3 4 5 6 7 8 9 10 11 12 13 14   98 97 96 95 94 93 92 91 90 89 88

King David

Retold by Catherine Storr
Pictures by Paul Crompton

Raintree Childrens Books
Milwaukee
Belitha Press Limited • London

Some time after David had killed Goliath, he lived in the King's palace. He became friends with Saul's son, Jonathan. Saul, the King, sent David to fight with the Philistines again.

When David returned from the battle, Saul heard the women singing, "Saul has killed his thousands, and David his ten thousands."

Then Saul was angry and jealous. The next time David played before him, Saul tried to kill him with a spear.

Jonathan said to his father, Saul, "David is good and wise and he has done you no harm. Why do you want to shed his innocent blood?"

Then Saul said, "No. He shall not be killed."

David came back to live in the King's palace, and Saul gave him his daughter, Michal, as a wife. But later Saul's anger and jealousy rose in him again, and while David was playing the harp, Saul threw a spear, meaning to pin him to the wall. But David slipped away and fled to his house.

Saul sent messengers to watch David's house at night. They meant to kill him in the morning. Michal, his wife, told him that he must escape, and she let him down out of a window in the darkness. Michal made a figure lying on David's bed, with a pillow of goat's hair for the head.

When Saul's messengers came the next morning, she told them David was ill. But Saul sent them back to fetch David in his bed, so that he could be killed. Then the messengers saw how Michal had tricked them.

9

For a long time, David had to stay in hiding because of Saul's anger against him. He stayed in the wilderness, and Saul gave Michal, David's wife, to be married to another man.

One night, David left the wilderness and came to the camp of Saul's army. He saw Saul asleep in a trench, with his spear stuck in the ground beside him. Abner, the captain of his army, was there too. David took the spear and a jar of water, and left Saul unharmed.

Then he went to the top of a high hill and called out, so that everyone could hear him, "Why do you pursue me with all these men?"

Saul said, "I have sinned. Come back to me, my son David."

David said, "Look! Here is your spear and your jar of water. I could have killed you while you slept, but I did not want to harm God's anointed King."

The war between Israel and the Philistines was still raging. Saul thought that the Philistines would be too strong for him, and when he asked God to guide him, God did not answer.

So Saul disguised himself and went to Endor, where a witch lived. He said, "I want to speak to the spirit of Samuel, who is dead."

The woman said, "The King has forbidden us to call up spirits. You will get me into trouble."

Saul promised that no trouble should come to her, and the woman called up the spirit of Samuel. But Samuel did not comfort Saul. He told Saul that he had disobeyed God, and that David would be the next King of Israel, instead of one of Saul's sons.

Soon after this, the Philistines were victorious. In one battle they killed Jonathan and two more of Saul's sons. When Saul knew of this he did not want to live any longer, and he killed himself. A messenger came to tell David that Saul and Jonathan were both dead. Then David wept and tore his clothes and mourned.

This was David's lament: "The beauty of Israel is slain upon the high places; how are the mighty fallen.

"Ye mountains of Gilboa, let there be no dew, neither let there be rain upon you nor fields of offerings, for there the shield of the mighty is vilely cast away.

"Saul and Jonathan were lovely and pleasant in their lives, and in their death they were not divided: they were swifter than eagles, they were stronger than lions.

"Ye daughters of Israel, weep over Saul, who clothed you in scarlet, with other delights, who put ornaments of gold upon your apparel.

"I am distressed for thee, my brother Jonathan; very pleasant hast thou been to me; thy love to me was wonderful, passing the love of women. How are the mighty fallen, and the weapons of war perished!"

Now that Saul was dead, Israel needed a new King. But the country was divided. David was made King of Judah and ruled at Hebron, but Abner, the captain of Saul's army, made one of Saul's other sons King of Gilead and of the Ashurites and the rest of Israel. There was a long war between these two sides. David became stronger and stronger, and Saul's son became weaker.

Abner and Saul's son quarrelled, so Abner sent secretly to David saying, "I will help you to become King of all Israel."

David said, "Very well. But you must let me have Michal, my wife."

When Abner brought Michal to David, David made a feast for him and let him go again in peace.

When Joab, the captain of David's army, heard of Abner's visit, he was furious. He said to David, "Why did you let Abner go away in peace? You know he came to spy on you, to find out your plans, so that he and his army could defeat us."

Then Joab sent messengers to ask Abner to meet him in Hebron, but he did not tell David.

When Abner came to the gate of the city, Joab took him aside as if he wanted to speak to him alone, but then he stabbed him in the heart.

David wept when he heard this. He said, "I am not guilty of this murder." He told all the people to mourn with him for Abner.

Not long after Abner's death, Saul's son was also murdered. Then all the tribes of Israel came to David at Hebron and said, "We are of your bone and flesh. You should rule over us all."

So David became King of all Israel. Now David brought the Ark of the Lord to Jerusalem. He made burnt sacrifices and he himself danced with all his might before the Ark.

His wife, Michal, looked out of her window and saw David dancing. She laughed and mocked him and said, "You were shameless, dancing in front of all the people."

God was angry with Michal for this, and she did not have any children.

One day, when David was walking on
the roof of his palace, he saw a very
beautiful woman in another house. He
asked who she was, and his servant said,
"That is Bathsheba, the wife of Uriah
the Hittite."

David wanted to have Bathsheba as
his own wife. He did a very mean thing.
He sent a message to Joab, the captain
of his army, saying, "Send Uriah the
Hittite to see me."

When Uriah had come to the palace, David wrote a letter to Joab and told Uriah to carry it back to the battlefront. The letter said, "Put Uriah in the front of the battle, with the bravest of men, so that he is certain to be killed."

Joab did as David had asked, and many of the bravest men were killed in the battle. Uriah died too. Joab sent messengers to David saying, "The enemy shot from the city wall and many men died. Your servant Uriah died too."

When Bathsheba heard that Uriah
had died, she mourned for him. But
after her mourning was over, David took
her as his wife, and they had a baby son.

Because of this sin of David's, God sent Nathan the prophet to tell him this story: "There were two men in a city. One was rich and one was poor. The rich man had herds of cattle and sheep, but the poor man had only one ewe lamb, which he loved. A traveler came to the city to be feasted.

But the rich man did not kill one of his own herd for the feast. He took away the ewe lamb from the poor man."

David was angry when he heard the story. He said, "The rich man was wicked. He deserved to die."

Nathan said, "You are that man. You had Uriah killed because you wanted his wife for yourself."

Then David saw that he had sinned, and God punished him by making Bathsheba's child fall sick. For days David would not eat; he prayed that his child might be made well again, but after seven days, the child died.

David's servants were surprised to see David wash himself and eat again. They said, "You went without food and wept while the child was alive. Now he is dead, why don't you still weep and fast?"

David said, "While the child was alive, God might have cured him. Now he is dead, there is no more to hope for. I shall go to him, but he shall not return to me."

After some time, Bathsheba bore David another son. His name was Solomon, and he would be the next ruler of Israel.

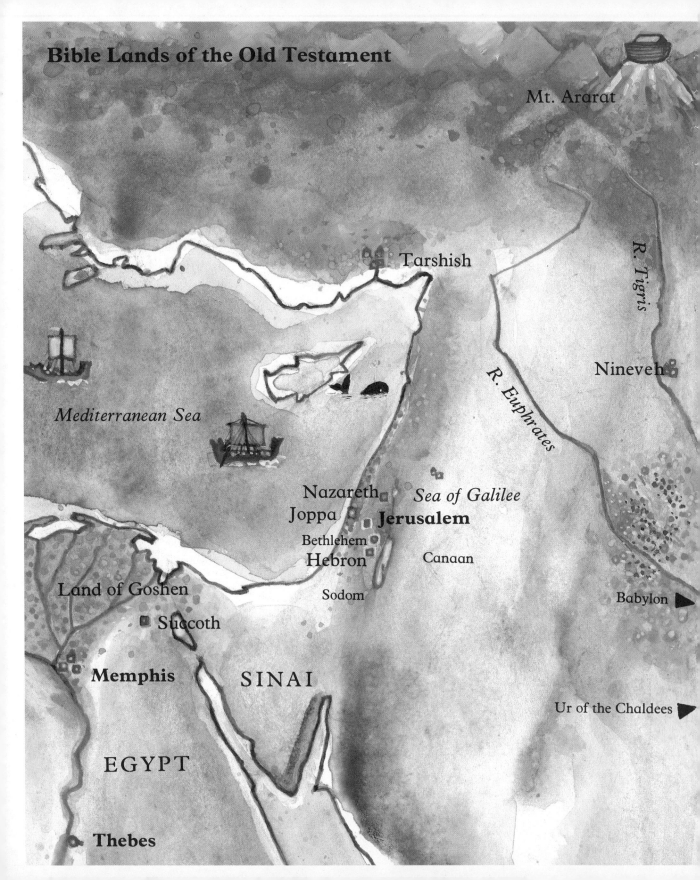

Bible Lands of the Old Testament

Mt. Ararat

Tarshish

R. Tigris

Nineveh

R. Euphrates

Mediterranean Sea

Nazareth

Sea of Galilee

Joppa

Jerusalem

Bethlehem

Hebron

Canaan

Sodom

Babylon ►

Land of Goshen

Succoth

Ur of the Chaldees ►

Memphis

S I N A I

EGYPT

Thebes